Georgia O'Keeffe

1999 DELUXE ENGAGEMENT BOOK

Catalog No. 99006

Published by Pomegranate, Box 6099, Rohnert Park, California 94927

© 1998 The Georgia O'Keeffe Foundation/Artists Rights Society, New York

■ ■ ■

Available in Canada from Firefly Books Ltd.,
3680 Victoria Park Avenue, Willowdale, Ontario M2H 3K1
Available in the U.K. and mainland Europe from Pomegranate Europe Ltd.,
Fullbridge House, Fullbridge, Maldon, Essex CM9 4LE, England
Available in Australia from Boobook Publications Pty. Ltd.,
P.O. Box 163 or Freepost 1, Tea Gardens 2324
Available in New Zealand from Randy Horwood Ltd.,
P.O. Box 32-077, Devonport, Auckland
Available in Asia (including the Middle East), Africa, and Latin America from
Pomegranate International Sales, 113 Babcombe Drive,
Thornhill, Ontario L3T 1M9, Canada

■ ■ ■

Pomegranate also publishes wall and pocket calendars for 1999 featuring the paintings of Georgia O'Keeffe. Our full-color catalog showing our wide selection of 1999 calendars is available for one dollar. We offer our other full-color catalogs (illustrating our notecards, boxed notes, notecard folios, postcards, books of postcards, address books, books of days, posters, art magnets, Knowledge Cards™, bookmarks, journals, and books) for nominal fees. For more information on obtaining catalogs and ordering, please write to Pomegranate, Box 6099, Rohnert Park, California 94927.

■ ■ ■

Front Cover: *White Pansy,* 1927
Oil on canvas, 19.8 x 76.5 cm (36¼ x 30 in.)
©The Cleveland Museum of Art. Bequest of Georgia O'Keeffe, 1987.130

■ ■ ■

Cover design by Harrah Argentine

All astronomical data supplied in this calendar are
expressed in Greenwich Mean Time (GMT).

☽	○	☾	●
FIRST QUARTER	FULL MOON	LAST QUARTER	NEW MOON

Georgia O'Keeffe (1887–1986) was the first female American painter to gain unanimous respect from both critics and the public the world over. Born near Sun Prairie, Wisconsin, a tiny village bordering the great north woods in the last century, O'Keeffe would become a giant of twentieth-century modern art—yet she carried the powerful simplicity of the prairie with her forever, maintaining an integrity in her art that reflected the integrity of her life. In intense and persistent pursuit of a subject, she tried to capture its essence—both in spirit and in form.

O'Keeffe's fame today rests upon subjects and devices she first employed in 1924, in her large flower paintings. In 1929, when she made her first trip to New Mexico, southwestern images began to take their place beside her abstracts and poppies. As the decades passed, perception of O'Keeffe became inseparable from the New Mexico landscape.

Known for her original approach to her art, O'Keeffe preferred not to limit her paintings by interpreting them, commenting, "I think I'd rather let the painting work for itself than help it with the word." Her eloquent work testifies to her powerful vision. This elegant calendar presents twenty paintings by one of the most revered and inventive of American artists.

Ram's Head, White Hollyhock—Hills, 1935

Oil on canvas, 76.2 x 91.4 cm (30 x 36 in.)
© Brooklyn Museum of Art 1992.11.28
Bequest of Edith and Milton Lowenthal

Boxing Day Observed (Canada)   m o n d a y

28 362

t u e s d a y

29 363

w e d n e s d a y

30 364

t h u r s d a y

31 365

New Year's Day   f r i d a y

1 1

s a t u r d a y

○ 2 2

s u n d a y

3 3

J A N U A R Y

S	M	T	W	T	F	S
					1	2
3	4	5	6	7	8	9
10	11	12	13	14	15	16
17	18	19	20	21	22	23
24	25	26	27	28	29	30
31						

January

monday

4 *4*

tuesday

5 *5*

wednesday

6 *6*

thursday

7 *7*

friday

8 *8*

saturday

9 *9*

sunday

10 *10*

JANUARY

S	M	T	W	T	F	S
					1	2
3	4	5	6	7	8	9
10	11	12	13	14	15	16
17	18	19	20	21	22	23
24	25	26	27	28	29	30
31						

monday

11 11

tuesday

12 12

wednesday

13 13

thursday

14 14

Martin Luther King Jr.'s Birthday

friday

15 15

saturday

16 16

sunday

● *17* 17

JANUARY

S	M	T	W	T	F	S
					1	2
3	4	5	6	7	8	9
10	11	12	13	14	15	16
17	18	19	20	21	22	23
24	25	26	27	28	29	30
31						

Sunflower, New Mexico, I, 1935

January

Martin Luther King Jr.'s Birthday Observed

monday

18 18

tuesday

19 19

wednesday

20 20

thursday

21 21

friday

22 22

saturday

23 23

sunday

☽ *24* 24

ANUARY

S	M	T	W	T	F	S
					1	2
3	4	5	6	7	8	9
10	11	12	13	14	15	16
17	18	19	20	21	22	23
24	25	26	27	28	29	30
31						

January

monday

25 **25**

tuesday

26 **26**

wednesday

27 **27**

thursday

28 **28**

friday

29 **29**

saturday

30 **30**

JANUARY

S	M	T	W	T	F	S
					1	2
3	4	5	6	7	8	9
10	11	12	13	14	15	16
17	18	19	20	21	22	23
24	25	26	27	28	29	30
31						

sunday

31 **31** ○

February

monday

1 32

tuesday

2 33

wednesday

3 34

thursday

4 35

friday

5 36

saturday

6 37

sunday

7 38

FEBRUARY

S	M	T	W	T	F	S
		1	2	3	4	5	6
7	8	9	10	11	12	13
14	15	16	17	18	19	20
21	22	23	24	25	26	27
28						

White Birch, 1925

Oil on canvas, 92 x 76.8 cm (36¼ x 30¼ in.)
Amon Carter Museum, Fort Worth, Texas
Partial and promised gift of Ruth Carter Stevenson, 1997.7

February

monday

☽ **8** 39

tuesday

9 40

wednesday

10 41

thursday

11 42

Lincoln's Birthday

friday

12 43

saturday

13 44

Valentine's Day

sunday

14 45

FEBRUARY

S	M	T	W	T	F	S
		1	2	3	4	5	6
7	8	9	10	11	12	13
14	15	16	17	18	19	20
21	22	23	24	25	26	27
28						

February

Presidents' Day

46 15

tuesday

47 16 ●

wednesday *Ash Wednesday*

48 17

thursday

49 18

friday

50 19

saturday

51 20

FEBRUARY

S	M	T	W	T	F	S
		1	2	3	4	5	6
7	8	9	10	11	12	13
14	15	16	17	18	19	20
21	22	23	24	25	26	27
28						

sunday

52 21

Washington's Birthday

monday

22 53

tuesday

☽ **23** 54

wednesday

24 55

thursday

25 56

friday

26 57

saturday

27 58

sunday

28 59

FEBRUARY

S	M	T	W	T	F	S
		1	2	3	4	5	6
7	8	9	10	11	12	13
14	15	16	17	18	19	20
21	22	23	24	25	26	27
28						

Red Cannas, 1927

Oil on canvas, 91.8 x 76.5 cm (36⅛ x 30⅛ in.)
Amon Carter Museum, Fort Worth, Texas, 1986.11

monday

1 60

tuesday

○ *2* 61

wednesday

3 62

thursday

4 63

friday

5 64

saturday

6 65

sunday

7 66

S	M	T	W	T	F	S
		1	2	3	4	5	6
7	8	9	10	11	12	13
14	15	16	17	18	19	20
21	22	23	24	25	26	27
28	29	30	31			

March

monday

67 *8*

tuesday

68 *9*

wednesday

69 *10* ☾

thursday

70 *11*

friday

71 *12*

saturday

72 *13*

sunday

73 *14*

monday

15 74

tuesday

16 75

St. *Patrick's Day*

wednesday

● ## 17 76

thursday

18 77

friday

19 78

saturday

20 79

sunday

21 80

Vernal Equinox 1:46 A.M. (GMT)

MARCH

S	M	T	W	T	F	S
		1	2	3	4	5	6
7	8	9	10	11	12	13
14	15	16	17	18	19	20
21	22	23	24	25	26	27
28	29	30	31			

Black Cross, New Mexico, 1929

Oil on canvas, 99.2 x 76.3 cm (39¹/₁₆ x 30¹/₁₆ in.)
Art Institute Purchase Fund, 1943.95
© *1998 The Art Institute of Chicago*

monday

22 81

tuesday

23 82

wednesday

☾ **24** 83

thursday

25 84

friday

26 85

saturday

27 86

Palm Sunday

sunday

28 87

MARCH

S	M	T	W	T	F	S
		1	2	3	4	5	6
7	8	9	10	11	12	13
14	15	16	17	18	19	20
21	22	23	24	25	26	27
28	29	30	31			

March
April

88 **29**

89 **30**

Passover (begins at sunset)

90 **31** ○

91 *1*

Good Friday

92 **2**

93 *3*

Easter Sunday

94 *4*

MARCH

S	M	T	W	T	F	S
		1	2	3	4	5	6
7	8	9	10	11	12	13
14	15	16	17	18	19	20
21	22	23	24	25	26	27
28	29	30	31			

Easter Monday (Canada)

monday

5 95

tuesday

6 96

wednesday

7 97

thursday

8 98

friday

☾ **9** 99

saturday

10 100

sunday

11 101

APRIL

S	M	T	W	T	F	S
				1	2	3
4	5	6	7	8	9	10
11	12	13	14	15	16	17
18	19	20	21	22	23	24
25	26	27	28	29	30	

Blue and Green Music, 1919

Oil on canvas, 57.2 x 47 cm (22½ x 18½ in.)
Alfred Stieglitz Collection, gift of Georgia O'Keeffe, 1969.835
© *1998 The Art Institute of Chicago*

April

monday

12 102

tuesday

13 103

wednesday

14 104

thursday

15 105

friday

● *16* 106

saturday

17 107

sunday

18 108

APRIL

S	M	T	W	T	F	S
				1	2	3
4	5	6	7	8	9	10
11	12	13	14	15	16	17
18	19	20	21	22	23	24
25	26	27	28	29	30	

Dark Tree Trunks, 1946

Oil on canvas, 101.6 x 76.2 cm (40 x 30 in.)
© Brooklyn Museum of Art 87.136.1
Bequest of Georgia O'Keeffe

April

monday

19 [109]

tuesday

20 [110]

wednesday

21 [111]

Earth Day

thursday

☽ 22 [112]

friday

23 [113]

saturday

24 [114]

sunday

25 [115]

April
May

tuesday

117 **27**

wednesday

118 **28**

thursday

119 **29**

friday

120 **30** ○

saturday

121 **1**

APRIL

S	M	T	W	T	F	S
				1	2	3
4	5	6	7	8	9	10
11	12	13	14	15	16	17
18	19	20	21	22	23	24
25	26	27	28	29	30	

sunday

122 **2**

monday

3 123

tuesday

4 124

Cinco de Mayo

wednesday

5 125

thursday

6 126

friday

7 127

saturday

☾ **8** 128

Mother's Day

sunday

9 129

MAY

S	M	T	W	T	F	S
						1
2	3	4	5	6	7	8
9	10	11	12	13	14	15
16	17	18	19	20	21	22
23	24	25	26	27	28	29
30	31					

Red and Pink Rocks and Teeth, 1938

monday

10 130

tuesday

11 131

wednesday

12 132

thursday

13 133

friday

14 134

Armed Forces Day

saturday

● *15* 135

sunday

16 136

MAY

S	M	T	W	T	F	S
						1
2	3	4	5	6	7	8
9	10	11	12	13	14	15
16	17	18	19	20	21	22
23	24	25	26	27	28	29
30	31					

White Shell with Red, 1938

Pastel on paper, 54.6 x 69.8 cm (21½ x 27½ in.)
Alfred Stieglitz Collection, bequest of Georgia O'Keeffe, 1987.250.5
© 1998 The Art Institute of Chicago

May

monday

17 137

tuesday

18 138

wednesday

19 139

thursday

20 140

friday

21 141

saturday

☽ *22* 142

sunday

23 143

MAY

S	M	T	W	T	F	S
						1
2	3	4	5	6	7	8
9	10	11	12	13	14	15
16	17	18	19	20	21	22
23	24	25	26	27	28	29
30	31					

May

MAY

monday   *Victoria Day (Canada)*

144 *24*

tuesday

145 *25*

wednesday

146 *26*

thursday

147 *27*

friday

148 *28*

saturday

149 *29*

MAY

S	M	T	W	T	F	S
						1
2	*3*	*4*	*5*	*6*	*7*	*8*
9	*10*	*11*	*12*	*13*	*14*	*15*
16	*17*	*18*	*19*	*20*	*21*	*22*
23	*24*	*25*	*26*	*27*	*28*	*29*
30	*31*					

sunday   *Memorial Day*

150 *30* ○

Memorial Day Observed

m o n d a y

$3I$ [151]

t u e s d a y

I [152]

w e d n e s d a y

2 [153]

t h u r s d a y

3 [154]

f r i d a y

4 [155]

s a t u r d a y

5 [156]

s u n d a y

6 [157]

JUNE

S	M	T	W	T	F	S
		1	2	3	4	5
6	7	8	9	10	11	12
13	14	15	16	17	18	19
20	21	22	23	24	25	26
27	28	29	30			

In the Patio No. 1, 1946

Oil on paper attached to board, 75.6 x 60.3 cm (29¾ x 23¾ in.)
© *San Diego Museum of Art*
Gift of Mr. and Mrs. Norton S. Walbridge

June

monday

☽ 7 158

tuesday

8 159

wednesday

9 160

thursday

10 161

friday

11 162

saturday

12 163

sunday

● 13 164

JUNE

S	M	T	W	T	F	S
		1	2	3	4	5
6	7	8	9	10	11	12
13	14	15	16	17	18	19
20	21	22	23	24	25	26
27	28	29	30			

June

monday   *Flag Day*

165   **14**

tuesday

166   **15**

wednesday

167   **16**

thursday

168   **17**

friday

169   **18**

saturday

170   **19**

sunday   *Father's Day*

171   **20**   ☽

June

Summer Solstice 7:49 P.M. (GMT)

monday

21 172

tuesday

22 173

wednesday

23 174

thursday

24 175

friday

25 176

saturday

26 177

sunday

27 178

JUNE

S	M	T	W	T	F	S
		1	2	3	4	5
6	7	8	9	10	11	12
13	14	15	16	17	18	19
20	21	22	23	24	25	26
27	28	29	30			

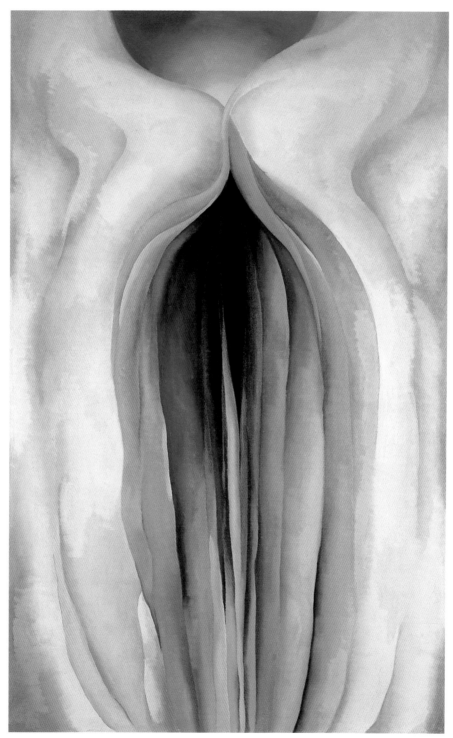

Gray Line with Black, Blue and Yellow, c.1923

Oil on canvas, 121.9 x 76.2 cm (48 x 30 in.)
© The Museum of Fine Arts Houston
Museum purchase with funds provided by the Agnes Cullen Arnold Endowment Fund, 77.331

June

July

monday

○ 28 179

tuesday

29 180

wednesday

30 181

Canada Day (Canada)   thursday

1 182

friday

2 183

saturday

3 184

Independence Day   sunday

4 185

JULY

S	M	T	W	T	F	S
				1	2	3
4	5	6	7	8	9	10
11	12	13	14	15	16	17
18	19	20	21	22	23	24
25	26	27	28	29	30	31

July

monday   *Independence Day Holiday*

186 **5**

tuesday

187 **6** ☾

wednesday

188 **7**

thursday

189 **8**

friday

190 **9**

saturday

191 **10**

JULY

S	M	T	W	T	F	S
				1	2	3
4	5	6	7	8	9	10
11	12	13	14	15	16	17
18	19	20	21	22	23	24
25	26	27	28	29	30	31

sunday

192 **11**

monday

12 193

tuesday

● *13* 194

wednesday

14 195

thursday

15 196

friday

16 197

saturday

17 198

sunday

18 199

JULY

S	M	T	W	T	F	S
				1	2	3
4	5	6	7	8	9	10
11	12	13	14	15	16	17
18	19	20	21	22	23	24
25	26	27	28	29	30	31

Dead Tree with a Pink Hill, 1945

Oil on canvas, 77.5 x 102.2 cm (30½ x 40¼ in.)
© 1998 The Cleveland Museum of Art
Bequest of Georgia O'Keeffe, 87.138

monday

19 200

tuesday

☽ *20* 201

wednesday

21 202

thursday

22 203

friday

23 204

saturday

24 205

sunday

25 206

JULY

S	M	T	W	T	F	S
				1	2	3
4	5	6	7	8	9	10
11	12	13	14	15	16	17
18	19	20	21	22	23	24
25	26	27	28	29	30	31

July
August

207 **26**

tuesday

208 **27**

wednesday

209 **28** ○

thursday

210 **29**

friday

211 **30**

saturday

212 **31**

JULY

S	M	T	W	T	F	S
				1	2	3
4	5	6	7	8	9	10
11	12	13	14	15	16	17
18	19	20	21	22	23	24
25	26	27	28	29	30	31

sunday

213 **1**

monday

2 214

tuesday

3 215

wednesday

☾ **4** 216

thursday

5 217

friday

6 218

saturday

7 219

sunday

8 220

AUGUST

S	M	T	W	T	F	S
1	2	3	4	5	6	7
8	9	10	11	12	13	14
15	16	17	18	19	20	21
22	23	24	25	26	27	28
29	30	31				

White Rose with Larkspur, No. 2

Oil on canvas, 101.6 x 76.2 cm (40 x 30 in.)
Courtesy The Museum of Fine Arts, Boston
Henry H. and Zoë Oliver Sherman Fund, 1980.207

monday

9 221

tuesday

10 222

wednesday

● **11** 223

thursday

12 224

friday

13 225

saturday

14 226

sunday

15 227

AUGUST

S	M	T	W	T	F	S
1	2	3	4	5	6	7
8	9	10	11	12	13	14
15	16	17	18	19	20	21
22	23	24	25	26	27	28
29	30	31				

August

monday

228 *16*

tuesday

229 *17*

wednesday

230 *18*

thursday

231 *19* ☽

friday

232 *20*

saturday

233 *21*

AUGUST

S	M	T	W	T	F	S
1	2	3	4	5	6	7
8	9	10	11	12	13	14
15	16	17	18	19	20	21
22	23	24	25	26	27	28
29	30	31				

sunday

234 *22*

August

monday

23 235

tuesday

24 236

wednesday

25 237

thursday

○ 26 238

friday

27 239

saturday

28 240

sunday

29 241

AUGUST

S	M	T	W	T	F	S
1	2	3	4	5	6	7
8	9	10	11	12	13	14
15	16	17	18	19	20	21
22	23	24	25	26	27	28
29	30	31				

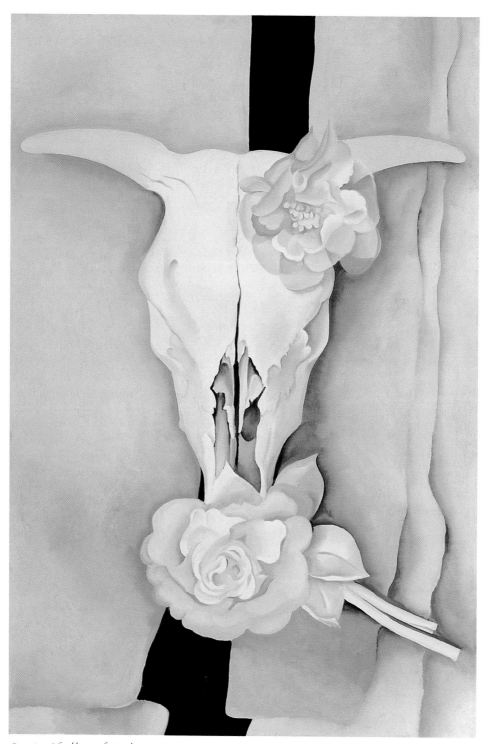

Cow's Skull with Calico Roses, 1932

Oil on canvas, 92.2 x 61.3 cm (36¼ x 24⅛ in.)
Gift of Georgia O'Keeffe, 1947.712
© 1998 The Art Institute of Chicago

monday

30 242

tuesday

31 243

wednesday

1 244

thursday

☾ *2* 245

friday

3 246

saturday

4 247

sunday

5 248

SEPTEMBER

S	M	T	W	T	F	S
			1	2	3	4
5	6	7	8	9	10	11
12	13	14	15	16	17	18
19	20	21	22	23	24	25
26	27	28	29	30		

White Trumpet Flower, 1932

Oil on canvas, 75.9 x 101.3 cm (29¾ x 39¾ in.)
© San Diego Museum of Art
Gift of Mrs. Inez Grant Parker in memory of Earle W. Grant, 1971.012

Labor Day (U.S. and Canada)

monday

6 249

tuesday

7 250

wednesday

8 251

thursday

● **9** 252

Rosh Hashanah (begins at sunset)

friday

10 253

saturday

11 254

sunday

12 255

SEPTEMBER

S	M	T	W	T	F	S
			1	2	3	4
5	6	7	8	9	10	11
12	13	14	15	16	17	18
19	20	21	22	23	24	25
26	27	28	29	30		

September

monday

256 13

tuesday

257 14

wednesday

258 15

thursday

259 16

friday

260 17 ☽

saturday

261 18

sunday   *Yom Kippur (begins at sunset)*

262 19

SEPTEMBER

S	M	T	W	T	F	S
			1	2	3	4
5	6	7	8	9	10	11
12	13	14	15	16	17	18
19	20	21	22	23	24	25
26	27	28	29	30		

September

monday

20 263

tuesday

21 264

wednesday

22 265

Autumnal Equinox 11:31 A.M. (GMT)

thursday

23 266

friday

24 267

saturday

○ ## 25 268

sunday

26 269

SEPTEMBER

S	M	T	W	T	F	S
			1	2	3	4
5	6	7	8	9	10	11
12	13	14	15	16	17	18
19	20	21	22	23	24	25
26	27	28	29	30		

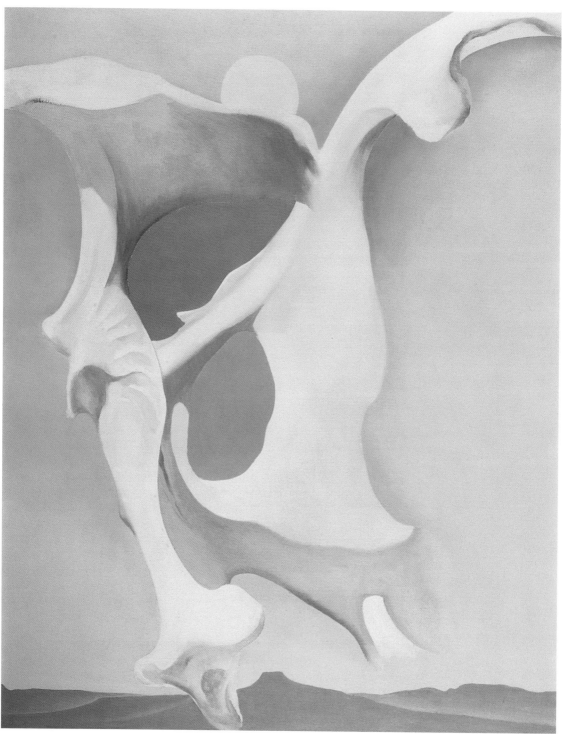

Pelvis with Moon, 1943

Oil on canvas, 76.2 x 61 cm (30 x 24 in.)
Collection of the Norton Museum of Art, West Palm Beach, Florida

monday

27 270

tuesday

28 271

wednesday

29 272

thursday

30 273

friday

1 274

saturday

☾ *2* 275

sunday

3 276

OCTOBER

S	M	T	W	T	F	S
					1	2
3	4	5	6	7	8	9
10	11	12	13	14	15	16
17	18	19	20	21	22	23
24	25	26	27	28	29	30
31						

Yellow Calla, 1926

Oil on fiberboard, 22.9 x 32.4 cm (9⅜ x 12¾ in.)
National Museum of American Art, Smithsonian Institution
Gift of the Woodward Foundation, 1978.34

October

monday

4 277

tuesday

5 278

wednesday

6 279

thursday

7 280

friday

8 281

saturday

 9 282

sunday

10 283

OCTOBER

S	M	T	W	T	F	S
					1	2
3	4	5	6	7	8	9
10	11	12	13	14	15	16
17	18	19	20	21	22	23
24	25	26	27	28	29	30
31						

October

---

monday

Columbus Day Observed
Thanksgiving Day (Canada)

284 **11**

---

tuesday

Columbus Day

285 **12**

---

wednesday

286 **13**

---

thursday

287 **14**

---

friday

288 **15**

---

saturday

289 **16**

OCTOBER

S	M	T	W	T	F	S
					1	2
3	4	5	6	7	8	9
10	11	12	13	14	15	16
17	18	19	20	21	22	23
24	25	26	27	28	29	30
31						

sunday

290 **17** ☽

October

monday

18 ²⁹¹

tuesday

19 ²⁹²

wednesday

20 ²⁹³

thursday

21 ²⁹⁴

friday

22 ²⁹⁵

saturday

23 ²⁹⁶

United Nations Day

sunday

○ ## 24 ²⁹⁷

OCTOBER

S	M	T	W	T	F	S
					1	2
3	4	5	6	7	8	9
10	11	12	13	14	15	16
17	18	19	20	21	22	23
24	25	26	27	28	29	30
31						

White Flower, 1929

Oil on canvas, 76.5 x 91.8 cm (30⅛ x 36⅛ in.)
© 1998 The Cleveland Museum of Art
Hinman B. Hurlbut Collection, 2162.1930

October

monday

25 ²⁹⁸

tuesday

26 ²⁹⁹

wednesday

27 ³⁰⁰

thursday

28 ³⁰¹

friday

29 ³⁰²

saturday

30 ³⁰³

Halloween

sunday

☾ ## 31 ³⁰⁴

OCTOBER

S	M	T	W	T	F	S
					1	2
3	4	5	6	7	8	9
10	11	12	13	14	15	16
17	18	19	20	21	22	23
24	25	26	27	28	29	30
31						

November

305 *1*

tuesday   *Election Day*

306 *2*

wednesday

307 *3*

thursday

308 *4*

friday

309 *5*

saturday

310 *6*

NOVEMBER

S	M	T	W	T	F	S
		1	2	3	4	5	6
7	8	9	10	11	12	13
14	15	16	17	18	19	20
21	22	23	24	25	26	27
28	29	30				

sunday

311 *7*

monday

● *8* 312

tuesday

9 313

wednesday

10 314

Veterans Day
Remembrance Day (Canada)

thursday

11 315

friday

12 316

saturday

13 317

sunday

14 318

NOVEMBER

S	M	T	W	T	F	S
	1	2	3	4	5	6
7	8	9	10	11	12	13
14	15	16	17	18	19	20
21	22	23	24	25	26	27
28	29	30				

Ranchos Church No. 1, c. 1929

Oil on canvas, 47.6 x 61 cm (18¾ x 24 in.)
Collection of the Norton Museum of Art, West Palm Beach, Florida

monday

15 319

tuesday

☽ 16 320

wednesday

17 321

thursday

18 322

friday

19 323

saturday

20 324

sunday

21 325

NOVEMBER

S	M	T	W	T	F	S
	1	2	3	4	5	6
7	8	9	10	11	12	13
14	15	16	17	18	19	20
21	22	23	24	25	26	27
28	29	30				

November

monday

326 **22**

tuesday

327 **23** ○

wednesday

328 **24**

thursday   *Thanksgiving Day*

329 **25**

friday

330 **26**

saturday

331 **27**

NOVEMBER

S	M	T	W	T	F	S
	1	2	3	4	5	6
7	8	9	10	11	12	13
14	15	16	17	18	19	20
21	22	23	24	25	26	27
28	29	30				

sunday

332 **28**

monday

☾ **29** ³³³

tuesday

30 ³³⁴

wednesday

1 ³³⁵

thursday

2 ³³⁶

Hanukkah (begins at sunset)

friday

3 ³³⁷

saturday

4 ³³⁸

sunday

5 ³³⁹

DECEMBER

S	M	T	W	T	F	S
			1	2	3	4
5	6	7	8	9	10	11
12	13	14	15	16	17	18
19	20	21	22	23	24	25
26	27	28	29	30	31	

White Pansy, 1927

Oil on canvas, 91.8 x 76.5 cm (36⅛ x 30⅛ in.)
© 1998 The Cleveland Museum of Art
Bequest of Georgia O'Keeffe, 1987.139

December

monday

6 340

tuesday

 7 341

wednesday

8 342

thursday

9 343

friday

10 344

saturday

11 345

sunday

12 346

DECEMBER

S	M	T	W	T	F	S
			1	2	3	4
5	6	7	8	9	10	11
12	13	14	15	16	17	18
19	20	21	22	23	24	25
26	27	28	29	30	31	

December

monday

347 13

tuesday

348 14

wednesday

349 15

thursday

350 16 ☽

friday

351 17

saturday

352 18

sunday

353 19

monday

20 354

tuesday

21 355

Winter Solstice 7:44 A.M. (GMT)

wednesday

○ 22 356

thursday

23 357

Christmas Day Holiday

friday

24 358

Christmas Day

saturday

25 359

Kwanzaa Begins
Boxing Day (Canada)

sunday

26 360

DECEMBER

S	M	T	W	T	F	S
			1	2	3	4
5	6	7	8	9	10	11
12	13	14	15	16	17	18
19	20	21	22	23	24	25
26	27	28	29	30	31	

December
January

monday

Boxing Day Observed (Canada)

361 **27**

tuesday

362 **28**

wednesday

363 **29** ☾

thursday

364 **30**

friday

365 **31**

saturday

New Year's Day 2000

1 **1**

JANUARY

S	M	T	W	T	F	S
						1
2	3	4	5	6	7	8
9	10	11	12	13	14	15
16	17	18	19	20	21	22
23	24	25	26	27	28	29
30	31					

sunday

2 **2**

Notes

1999

JANUARY

S	M	T	W	T	F	S
					1	2
3	4	5	6	7	8	9
10	11	12	13	14	15	16
17	18	19	20	21	22	23
24	25	26	27	28	29	30
31						

FEBRUARY

S	M	T	W	T	F	S
	1	2	3	4	5	6
7	8	9	10	11	12	13
14	15	16	17	18	19	20
21	22	23	24	25	26	27
28						

MARCH

S	M	T	W	T	F	S
	1	2	3	4	5	6
7	8	9	10	11	12	13
14	15	16	17	18	19	20
21	22	23	24	25	26	27
28	29	30	31			

APRIL

S	M	T	W	T	F	S
				1	2	3
4	5	6	7	8	9	10
11	12	13	14	15	16	17
18	19	20	21	22	23	24
25	26	27	28	29	30	

MAY

S	M	T	W	T	F	S
						1
2	3	4	5	6	7	8
9	10	11	12	13	14	15
16	17	18	19	20	21	22
23	24	25	26	27	28	29
30	31					

JUNE

S	M	T	W	T	F	S
		1	2	3	4	5
6	7	8	9	10	11	12
13	14	15	16	17	18	19
20	21	22	23	24	25	26
27	28	29	30			

JULY

S	M	T	W	T	F	S
				1	2	3
4	5	6	7	8	9	10
11	12	13	14	15	16	17
18	19	20	21	22	23	24
25	26	27	28	29	30	31

AUGUST

S	M	T	W	T	F	S
1	2	3	4	5	6	7
8	9	10	11	12	13	14
15	16	17	18	19	20	21
22	23	24	25	26	27	28
29	30	31				

SEPTEMBER

S	M	T	W	T	F	S
			1	2	3	4
5	6	7	8	9	10	11
12	13	14	15	16	17	18
19	20	21	22	23	24	25
26	27	28	29	30		

OCTOBER

S	M	T	W	T	F	S
					1	2
3	4	5	6	7	8	9
10	11	12	13	14	15	16
17	18	19	20	21	22	23
24	25	26	27	28	29	30
31						

NOVEMBER

S	M	T	W	T	F	S
	1	2	3	4	5	6
7	8	9	10	11	12	13
14	15	16	17	18	19	20
21	22	23	24	25	26	27
28	29	30				

DECEMBER

S	M	T	W	T	F	S
			1	2	3	4
5	6	7	8	9	10	11
12	13	14	15	16	17	18
19	20	21	22	23	24	25
26	27	28	29	30	31	

2000

JANUARY

S	M	T	W	T	F	S
						1
2	3	4	5	6	7	8
9	10	11	12	13	14	15
16	17	18	19	20	21	22
23	24	25	26	27	28	29
30	31					

FEBRUARY

S	M	T	W	T	F	S
		1	2	3	4	5
6	7	8	9	10	11	12
13	14	15	16	17	18	19
20	21	22	23	24	25	26
27	28	29				

MARCH

S	M	T	W	T	F	S
			1	2	3	4
5	6	7	8	9	10	11
12	13	14	15	16	17	18
19	20	21	22	23	24	25
26	27	28	29	30	31	

APRIL

S	M	T	W	T	F	S
						1
2	3	4	5	6	7	8
9	10	11	12	13	14	15
16	17	18	19	20	21	22
23	24	25	26	27	28	29
30						

MAY

S	M	T	W	T	F	S
	1	2	3	4	5	6
7	8	9	10	11	12	13
14	15	16	17	18	19	20
21	22	23	24	25	26	27
28	29	30	31			

JUNE

S	M	T	W	T	F	S
				1	2	3
4	5	6	7	8	9	10
11	12	13	14	15	16	17
18	19	20	21	22	23	24
25	26	27	28	29	30	

JULY

S	M	T	W	T	F	S
						1
2	3	4	5	6	7	8
9	10	11	12	13	14	15
16	17	18	19	20	21	22
23	24	25	26	27	28	29
30	31					

AUGUST

S	M	T	W	T	F	S
		1	2	3	4	5
6	7	8	9	10	11	12
13	14	15	16	17	18	19
20	21	22	23	24	25	26
27	28	29	30	31		

SEPTEMBER

S	M	T	W	T	F	S
					1	2
3	4	5	6	7	8	9
10	11	12	13	14	15	16
17	18	19	20	21	22	23
24	25	26	27	28	29	30

OCTOBER

S	M	T	W	T	F	S
1	2	3	4	5	6	7
8	9	10	11	12	13	14
15	16	17	18	19	20	21
22	23	24	25	26	27	28
29	30	31				

NOVEMBER

S	M	T	W	T	F	S
			1	2	3	4
5	6	7	8	9	10	11
12	13	14	15	16	17	18
19	20	21	22	23	24	25
26	27	28	29	30		

DECEMBER

S	M	T	W	T	F	S
					1	2
3	4	5	6	7	8	9
10	11	12	13	14	15	16
17	18	19	20	21	22	23
24	25	26	27	28	29	30
31						

Personal Information

Name _____

Address _____

City _____

State _____

Zip _____

Phone _____

Fax _____

E-mail _____

In case of emergency, please notify:

Name _____

Address _____

City _____

State _____

Zip _____

Phone _____

Medical Information:

Physician's Name _____

Physician's Phone _____

Health insurance company _____

Plan number _____

Allergies _____

Other _____

Other Information:

Driver's license number _____

Car insurance company _____

Policy number _____